DESIGN & LIGHT

THREE-DIMENSIONAL COLOR EFFECTS AND PATTERNS IN ABSTRACT DESIGN

ARRANGED AND EDITED BY WOLFGANG HAGENEY

BELVEDERE

EDITION BELVEDERE CO. LTD., ROME - MILAN (ITALY)

IMPRESSUM

PUBLICATION BY
EDITION BELVEDERE CO.LTD.
ROME-MILAN (ITALY)

© COPYRIGHT 1988
BY EDITION BELVEDERE CO.LTD.

A747

THIS VOLUME WAS FIRST PUBLISHED
1988

PRINTED IN ITALY BY
STUDIO TIPOGRAFICO, ROME/ITALY
FILMS & PHOTOLITHOGRAPHY BY
BELVEDERE LABORATORIES, ROME/ITALY
LASER TYPE SETTING BY
COMP.LAB BELVEDERE, ROME/ITALY

LAYOUT & STYLING BY
STUDIO BELVEDERE, ROME/ITALY

ART DIRECTION: HWH & BVR
ARTWORK & GRAPHIC DESIGN BY
STUDIO BELVEDERE, ROME

PRINT PRODUCTION: MARCELLO CARMELLINI
STUDIO PRODUCTION: ROSA LENGSFELD
EDITOR & PUBLISHER: WOLFGANG H. HAGENEY

"DESIGNER'S NOTEBOOK"® is part
of the BELVEDERE PUBLICATIONS INTERNTL.
where also are published the
BELVEDERE-DESIGN-BOOKS, DESIGN-BOOKS-
PAPERBACKS, CULTURE DESIGN-BOOKS®,
ARCHI-BOOKS®, CAD-BOOKS®, REF.-BOOKS®,
GRAFIX®, PAGE-LAYOUT-SYSTEM®, BELVUE®
LOGO-TYPE-FACES®, MIX-MEDIA®, STYL®,
IMAGE-BANK®
® Registred Trademark

The BELVEDERE PUBLICATIONS
are available through the general booktrade, art-
supply shops, special agents or exclusively through
the BELVEDERE-DESIGN-CLUB INTERNATIONAL
by international mail order system (for members only)

The publications are also available by subscription or
by standing order directly from the publishing house.
For any information, for membership or subscription,
please write to:

EDITION BELVEDERE CO.LTD.
00196 ROME/ITALY, PIAZZALE FLAMINIO, 19
TEL. (06) 360.44.88 / FAX (06) 360.29.60
TELEX: 621600 PPRMMZ I-3604488

ISBN 88-7070-063-1

INFORMATION

A Symphony conductor hastens to his podium, lifts his baton — a gesture followed by each musician as he puts his instrument in place and straightens his body — and breaks the moment of silent suspense with the first motion of his hand. We follow his graceful movements which direct the flow of music, now coaxing forth the delicate notes of the solo violin and now letting loose an entire flood of tones. We observe the shadows cast by the swaying of his body, by the movement of his hands — shadows which are all in harmony with the music and which are necessarily synonymous with it.

Again, we stop to observe a brass band on parade. Each and every member of the band performs his own peculiar set of movements adapted to the instrument played. The motions of all — the cornetist, the drummer, the tuba player, end even the drum major — are in tune. And the shadows of these movements are its corresponding silhouettes in rhythmic beats of music.

So it is with everything about us. The moving shadows of an airplane upon the earth's surface, the momentary silhouettes of people passing on the street, the checkerboard-pattern of rustling leaves upon the sunlit grass — all these shadows are the rhythmic counterparts of their objects. The same truth holds for anything in movement or for any swaying light upon a stationary object. It is the romance of light and shade translated into pattern and color.

The photographer is the modern exponent of this theory of light and shade; he has learned to use this cultural pattern, inherent in our consciousness, for artistic purposes. He knows, for instance, that, just as we visualize an automobile when we hear the blare of a horn, or an airplane when its hum reaches our ears, so we mentally image a tree by its shade upon the grass, the human form by its shadow cast upon the wall. So spontaneous and instinctive is our reaction to this pattern of light and shade that we are generally quite unconscious of its really vital significance, of its beauty of outline and color.

We do not realize that much of the appeal of the plastic arts, of architecture, of the world of nature, is a result of the presence of the third dimension, depth, without which there can be no contrast of light and shade, no play of shades and shadows. A two-dimensional existence is unthinkable; we need the half-lights and shade-colors in life.

Indeed, so important is this co-relation of object and shadow that mankind has confounded the actual and its shade until the two have come to symbolize to all peoples the Real and the Ideal, the Aristotelian and Platonic aspects of life. An excellent example of this symbolic use is Hans Christian Anderson's famous folk-tale of the Shadow that became a Man. Who can say whether the world which we see is the object of our thought or the shadow of it?

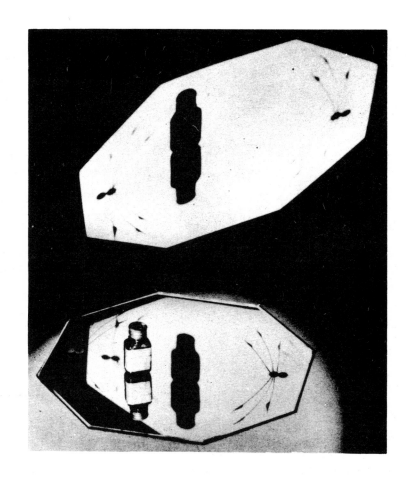

Work Sheet, Photographs

FIGURE A—Basic design of lamp bulb and its shadow as illustrated on Plate 8-A. The shadow in this case overlaps and coincides. Two forms of the lamp bulb with their coinciding shadows form the patterns in color.

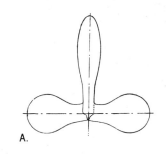

A.

FIGURE B—Basic design of lamp bulb and its shadow as illustrated on Plate 9-A. This pattern is the opposite of Plate 8-A in that the overlapping circular part of the lamp bulb coincides forming a pattern with two shadows; only one bulb and two stems of the lamp bulb.

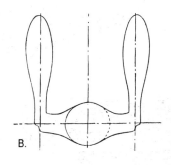

B.

FIGURE C—Basic design of match box and ping-pong ball together with their shadows producing new creations other than those illustrated on Plate 15-A. This is a typical illustration of the sphere of the ping-pong ball overlapping itself, forming one circle with rectangular patterns and shadows.

FIGURE D—Basic design of match box and ping-pong ball which is the same as Figure C with the exception of introduced lines of perspective.

FIGURE E—Basic design of match box and ping-pong ball which may be used to create a vertical or horizontal pattern; no perspective introduced.

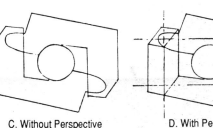

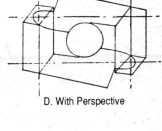

C. Without Perspective

D. With Perspective

FIGURE F—Basic design of match box and ping-pong ball the same as in Figure E with the additional lines of perspective.

FIGURE G—Basic design of match box and ping-pong ball in which the rectangular match box overlaps the ping-pong ball four times. The pattern already becomes complicated. If done on a large scale, the lines of perspective may be introduced. In the small scale pattern it would be almost impossible to use lines in perspective.

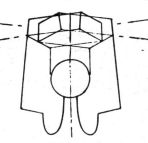

E. Without Perspective

F. With Perspective

FIGURE C-G, Inclusive—A variety of the use of one photograph of the match box and ping-pong ball into a given number of basic patterns. These again may be multiplied on each sheet of illustrations in the same manner as the plate of color designs on Plate 15-A; thus making a multiple number of different patterns from a given object or objects.

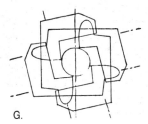

G.

1

Historic ornament is derived primarily from two sources: nature and geometric design. Flora and Fauna, together with geometry, are the origins for nearly all forms of historic ornament. To these two sources of design must be added the ever present guiding forces of human ingenuity and imagination. Those factors account for all designs that have been created through the ages.

In the Twenties several portfolios of color plates, have been published, that feature modern design emphasizing three-dimensional color effects and some abstract designs. These portfolios were produced by such eminent artists as Edouard Benedictus, A. Garcelon, M. Serge Gladky, and others. Yet none of these portfolios has shown how to create any given pattern; the possible sources of these patterns in color are not explained by any method or procedure....

EletricIronDesign

PLATE 1-A. Electric Iron Design

9

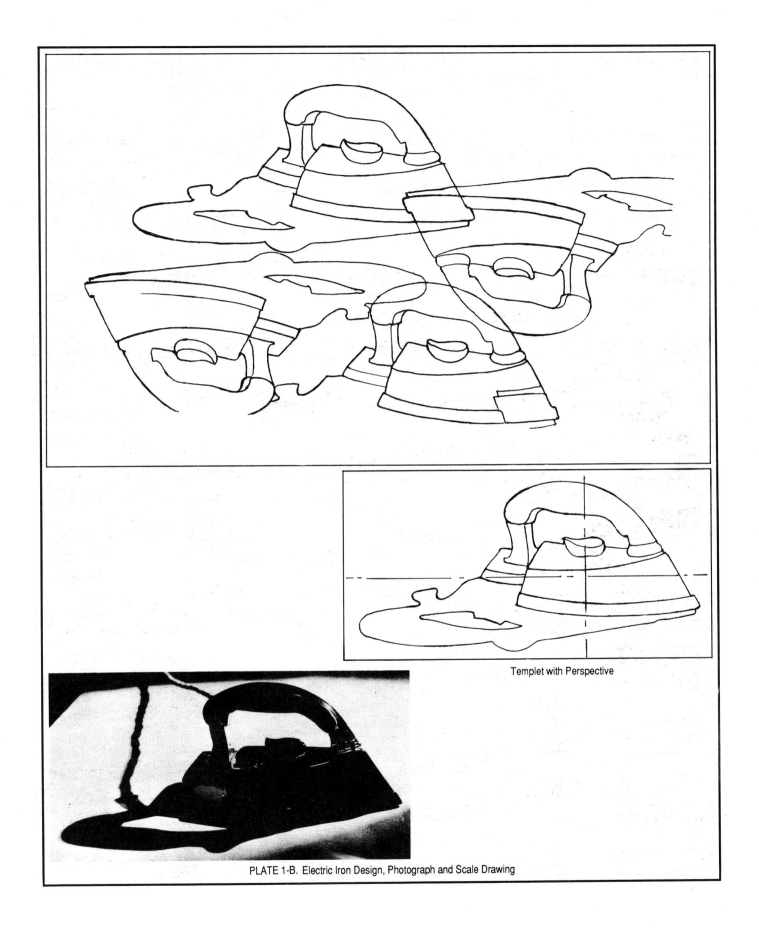

Templet with Perspective

PLATE 1-B. Electric Iron Design, Photograph and Scale Drawing

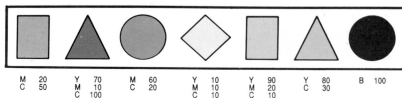

M 20	Y 70	M 60	Y 10	Y 90	Y 80	B 100
C 50	M 10	C 20	M 10	M 20	C 30	
	C 100		C 10	C 10		

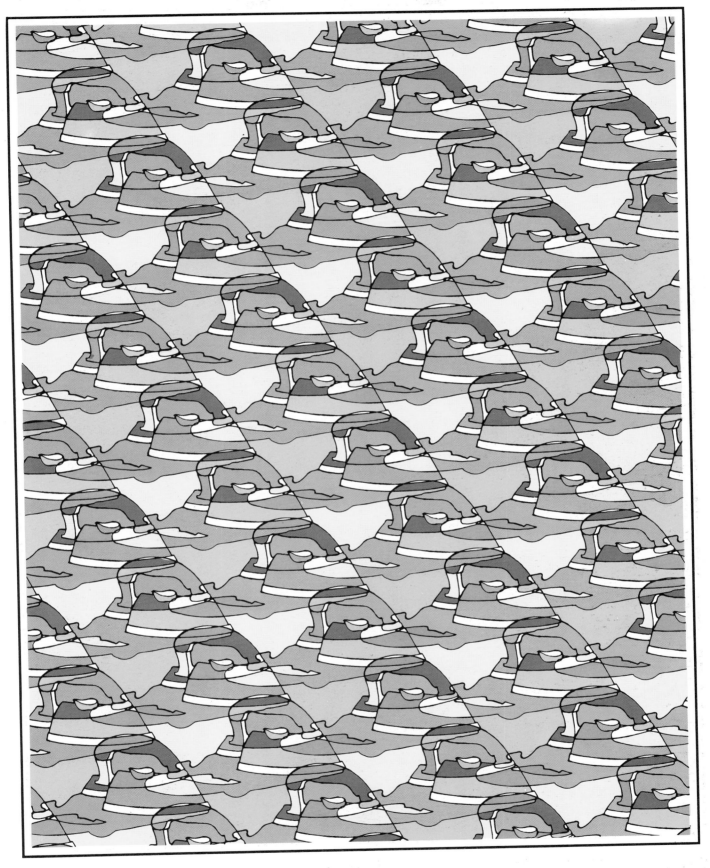

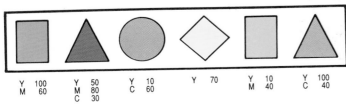

Y 100   Y 50   Y 10   Y 70   Y 10   Y 100
M 60   M 80   C 60   M 40   C 40
         C 30

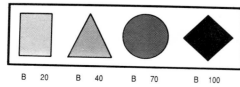

B   20   B   40   B   70   B   100

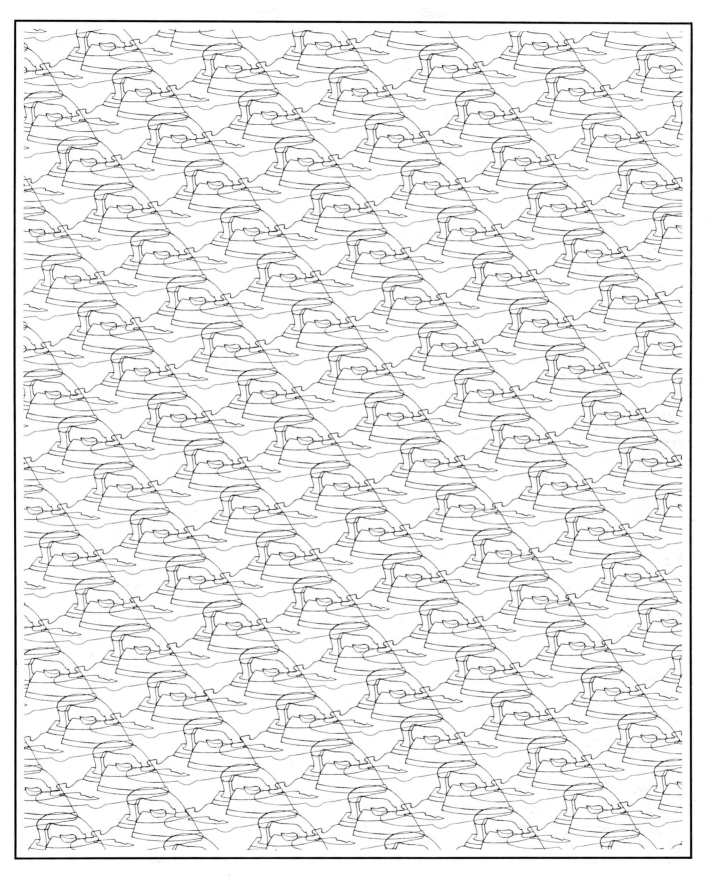

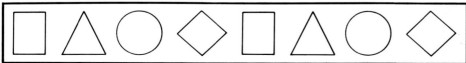

2

Artists throughout time developed ingenious designs based upon geometry and, more especially, upon natural forms. An additional source of design, light and shadows in nature, has been used but heretofore has not been systematically explained. The very definition of the word "shadows" compels a consistency between a lighted object and its shade. Thus, by the method developed through these plates, a new romance in patterns and designs is evolved. These are created not from nature but rather from objects and shadows of manufactured articles exemplifying an age of power and industry.

The three-dimensional patterns as illustrated in other publications represent the forms of cubes, rectangles, circles, and spheres in their structural combinations and with their shadows as the third dimension in color....

S h o e D e s i g n

PLATE 2-A. Shoe Design

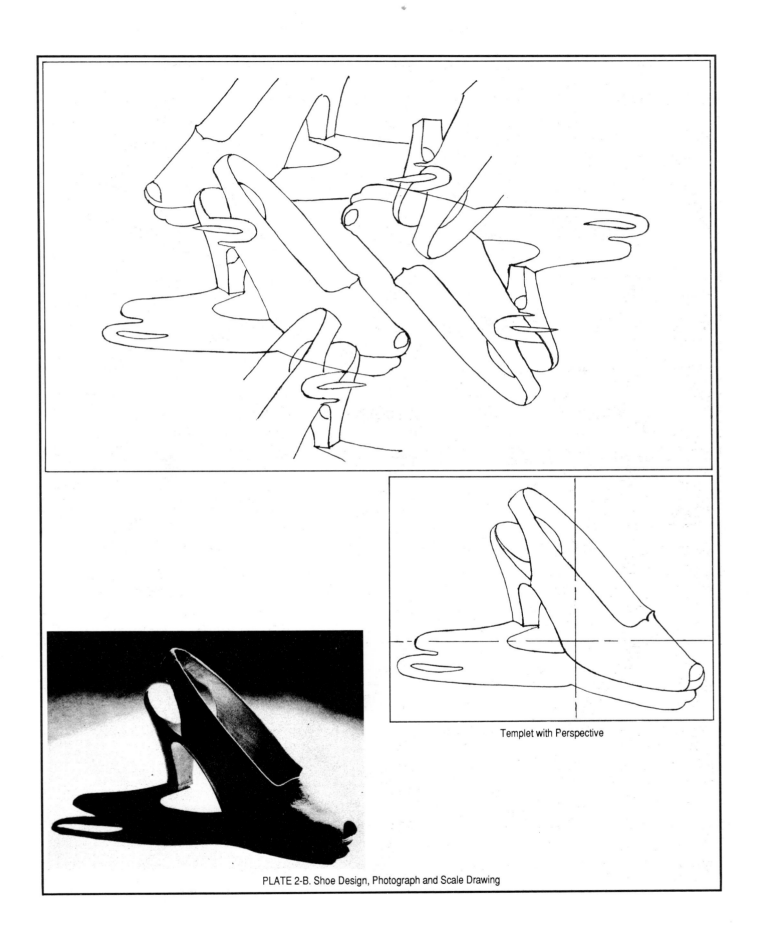

Templet with Perspective

PLATE 2-B. Shoe Design, Photograph and Scale Drawing

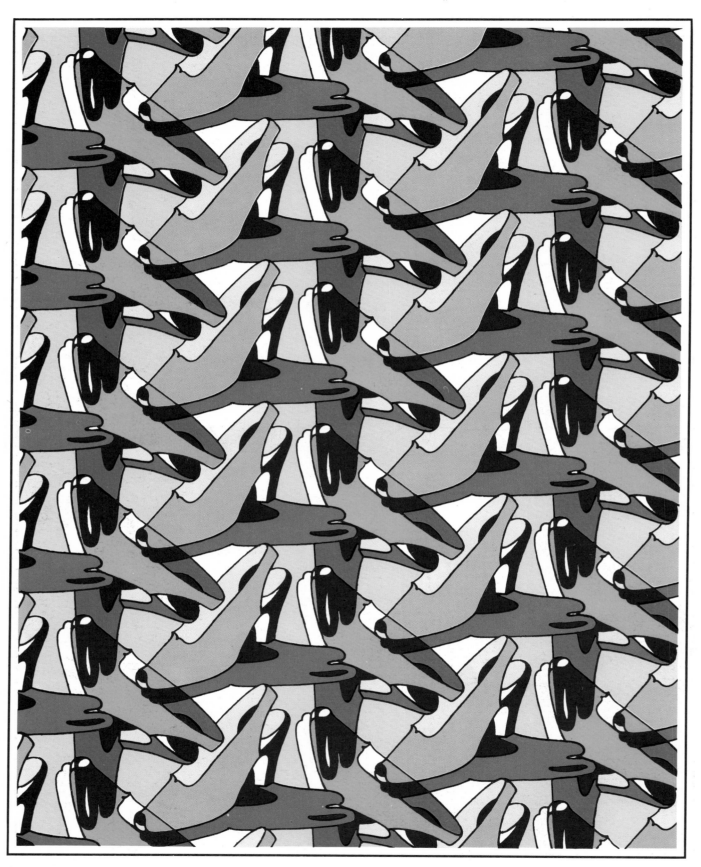

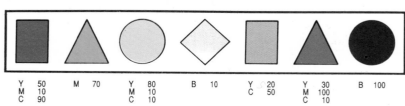

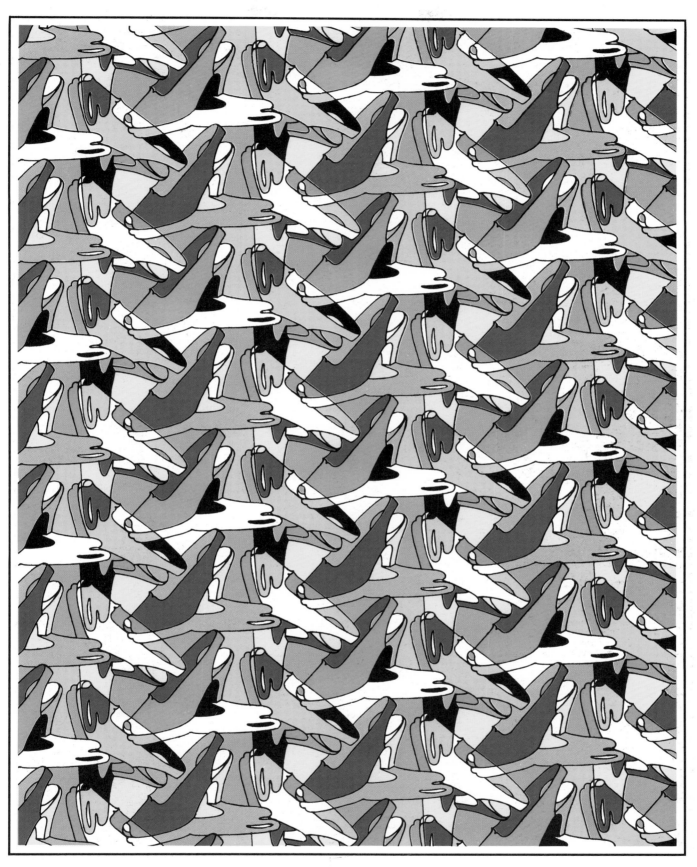

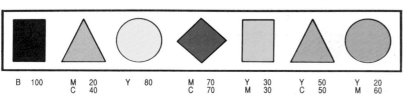

B 100   M 20   Y 80   M 70   Y 30   Y 50   Y 20
C 40   C 70   M 30   C 50   M 60

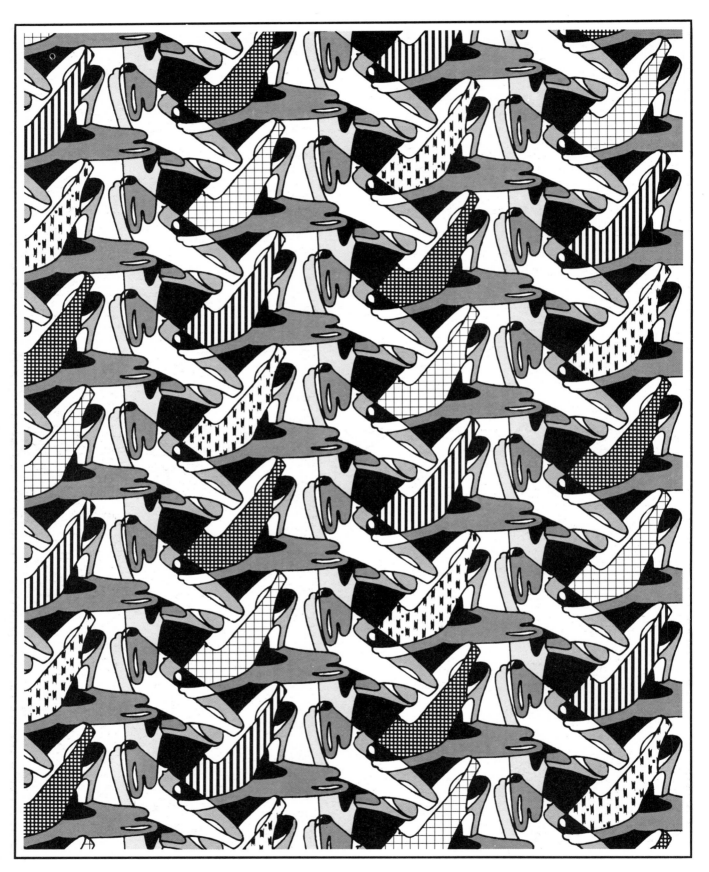

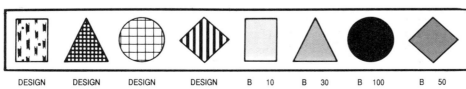

DESIGN   DESIGN   DESIGN   DESIGN   B 10   B 30   B 100   B 50

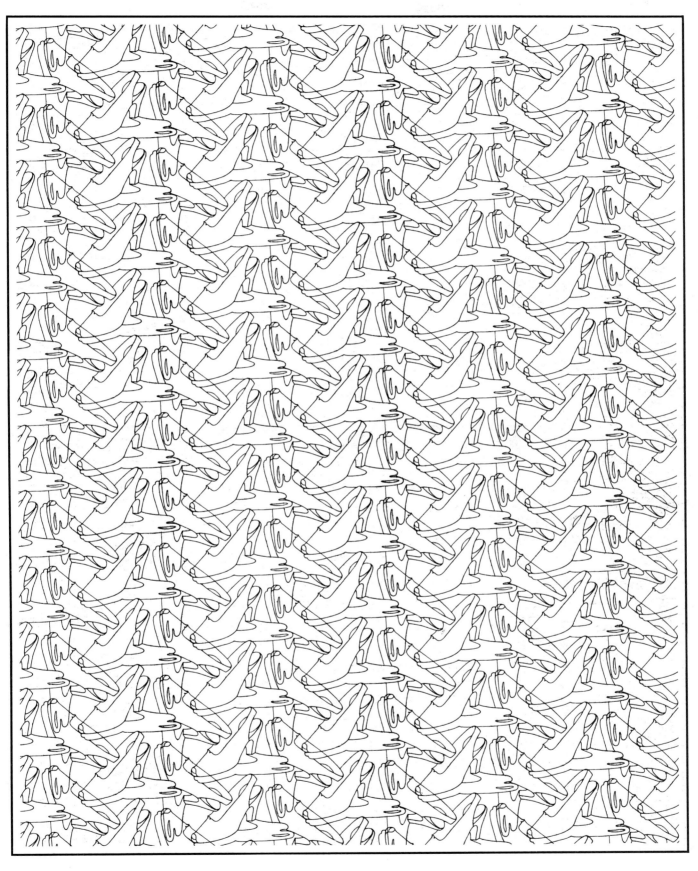

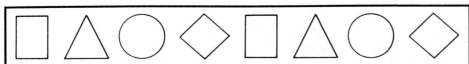

3

In the present book the objects and their shadows are treated as equal values because, when desired, the outlines of the shadows or of the objects create patterns completely lacking in any suggestion of their real form.

The play of light and shade is always an essential factor for color in architecture, painting, sculpture, engineering, and as well as the industrial arts; without it photography would not exist. However, the form of an object with its play of light and shade from a point of view of design has been seldom used by the artist in his creation of pattern. When used, light and shade have been determined usually by sunlight. The possibilities in pattern evolved through light and shade by artificial illumination have not been used or realized. Artists or laymen studying these plates will observe that they are all based on a definite method of creating designs....

Gear Design

PLATE 3-A. Gear Design

A

B

C

D

25

Templet with Perspective

PLATE 3-B. Gear Design, Photograph and Scale Drawing

27

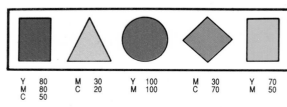

Y 80   M 30   Y 100   M 30   Y 70
M 80   C 20   M 100   C 70   M 50
C 50

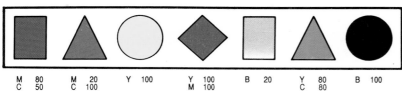
29

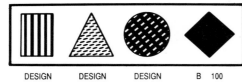

DESIGN   DESIGN   DESIGN   B   100

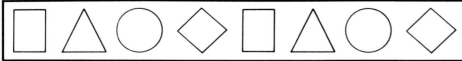

4

This method allows unlimited originality, for any product may be decorated with designs created by its own shape and shadows. The word "shadows" is correct because this method permits the use of one source of light casting one shadow or of multiple sources casting many shadows simultaneously around one object.

Shadows as photographed throughout these plates have been cast by artificial illumination. This is emphasized because there is a marked difference between shadows cast by sunlight and those cast by artificial lighting. Shadows cast by sunlight become longer or shorter; however, they are never any wider than the objects from which the shadows are cast. This is due to the great distance between the object and the sun. The parallel rays of sunlight make the shadow the same width as the object casting the shadow and, if anything, it appears to diminish rather than retain its own width....

H a t D e s i g n

A

B

C

D

E

F

PLATE 4-A. Hat Design

G

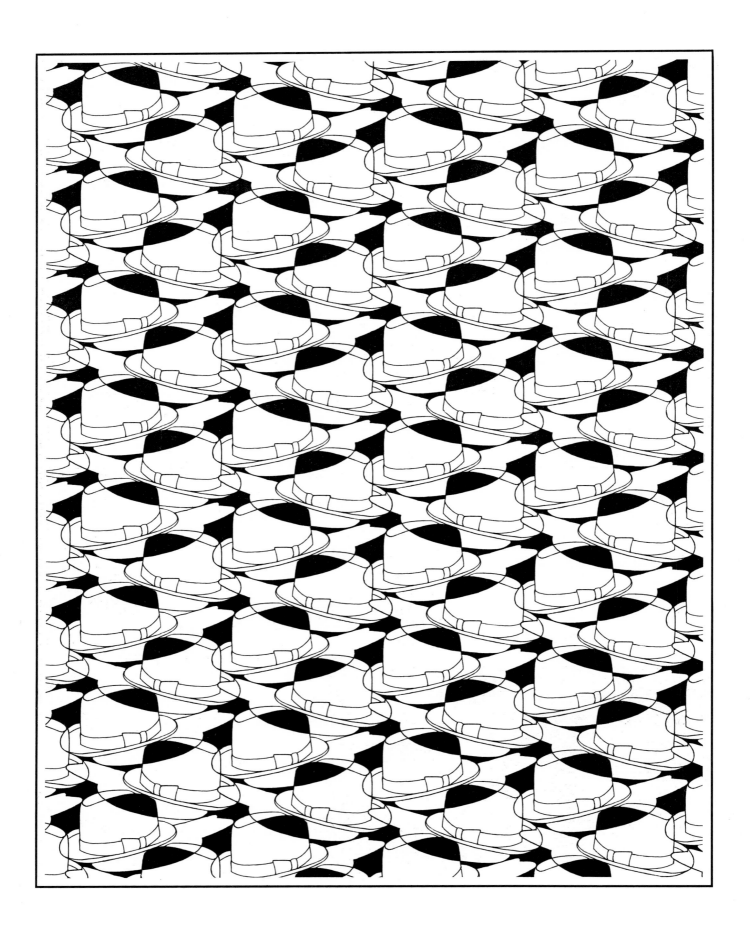

Templet with Perspective

PLATE 4-B. Hat Design, Photograph and Scale Drawing

35

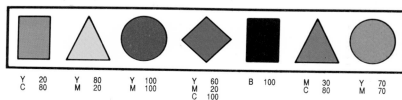

Y 20	Y 80	Y 100	Y 60	B 100	M 30	Y 70
C 80	M 20	M 100	M 20		C 80	M 70
			C 100			

36

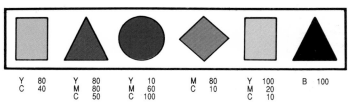

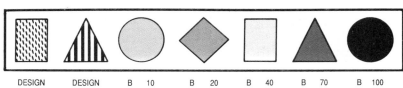

DESIGN   DESIGN   B 10   B 20   B 40   B 70   B 100

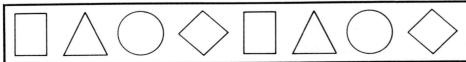

5

In artificial illumination the shadows become longer or shorter and also wider than the objects casting the shadows, since the presence of the source of light is near the object. Through the use of artificial illumination, the light source can be controlled; thereby the type of shadow most desired is achieved. A spotlight will give a much clearer outline of shadows for use in designing although any artificial light will serve the purpose.

The designs are methodically evolved by simply overlaying a series of combined silhouettes of the object and its shadow. This method results in unusual geometric shapes and forms that could not be evolved mathematically and probably would never be creations of the imagination without direction. By using the object and its shadow and then losing the identities of the two with overlays or superimpositions together with intervening spaces, there is always a full page of some geometric field pattern....

LockWasherDesign

PLATE 5-A. Lock Washer Design

A

B

C

D

E

F

G

41

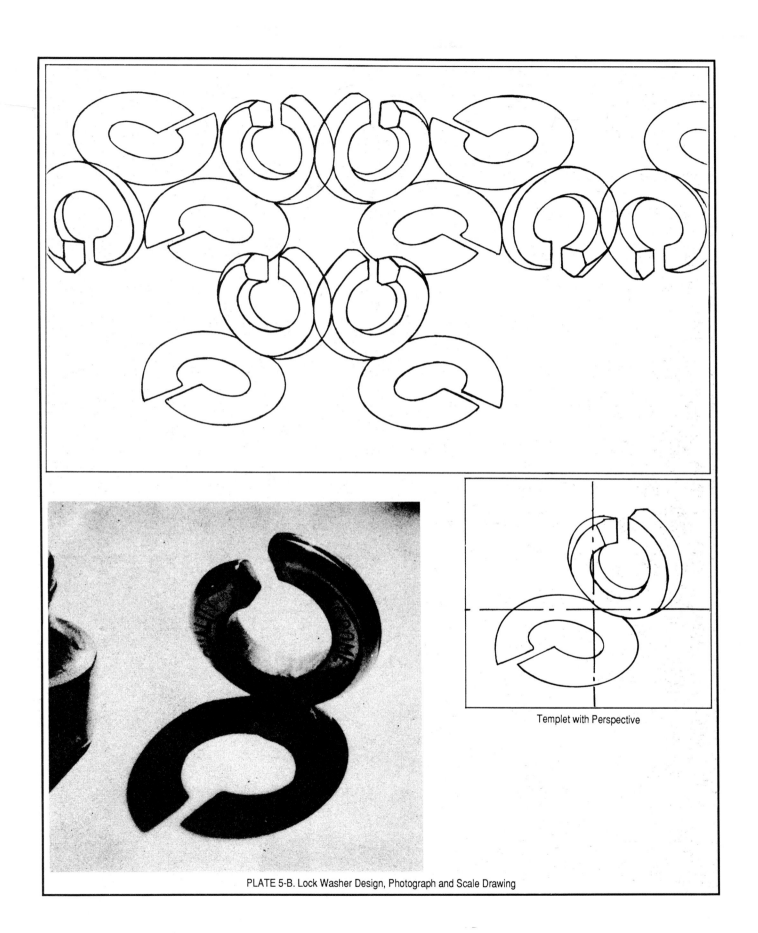

Templet with Perspective

PLATE 5-B. Lock Washer Design, Photograph and Scale Drawing

6

Elimination of the object itself or of part of it, or the deletion of part or all of the shadow, produces most interesting patterns in abstract design. The separation of patterns is accomplished through the application of color. Patterns may be made to read one way by retaining the object and its shadow in the same position of overlays or superimpositions such as some of the designs in wall patterns; in this manner the form of the object is retained. By an overlay of the object in an inverted position, the pattern will read both ways; thus the object creating the pattern loses its identity.

Plates of design with varied lines of direction: for the horizontal and vertical effects see Plates 15-A, B and 9-A, B; diagonal patterns are found on Plates 13-A, B and 14-A, B and 8-A, B; staggered patterns on Plates 10-A, B....

LockWasherDesign

PLATE 6-A. Lock Washer Design

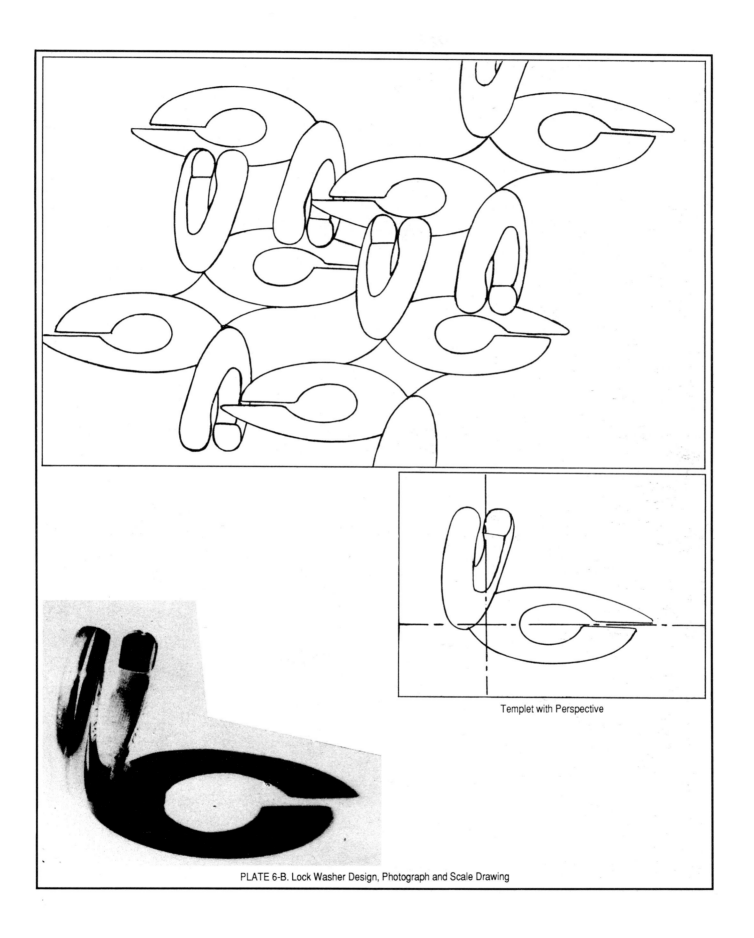

Templet with Perspective

PLATE 6-B. Lock Washer Design, Photograph and Scale Drawing

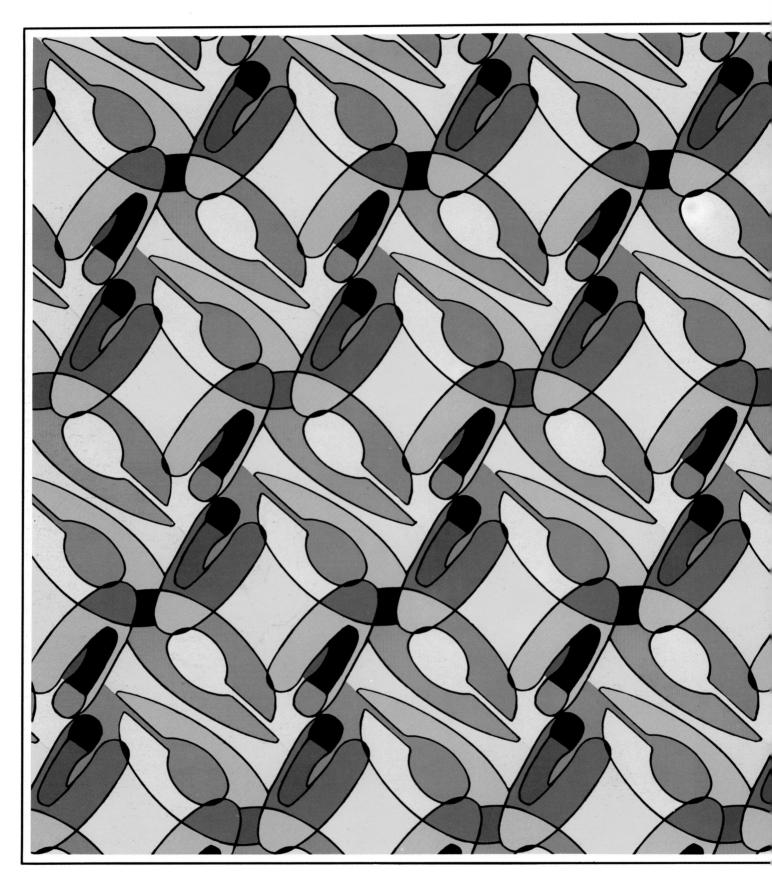

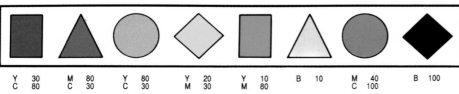

49

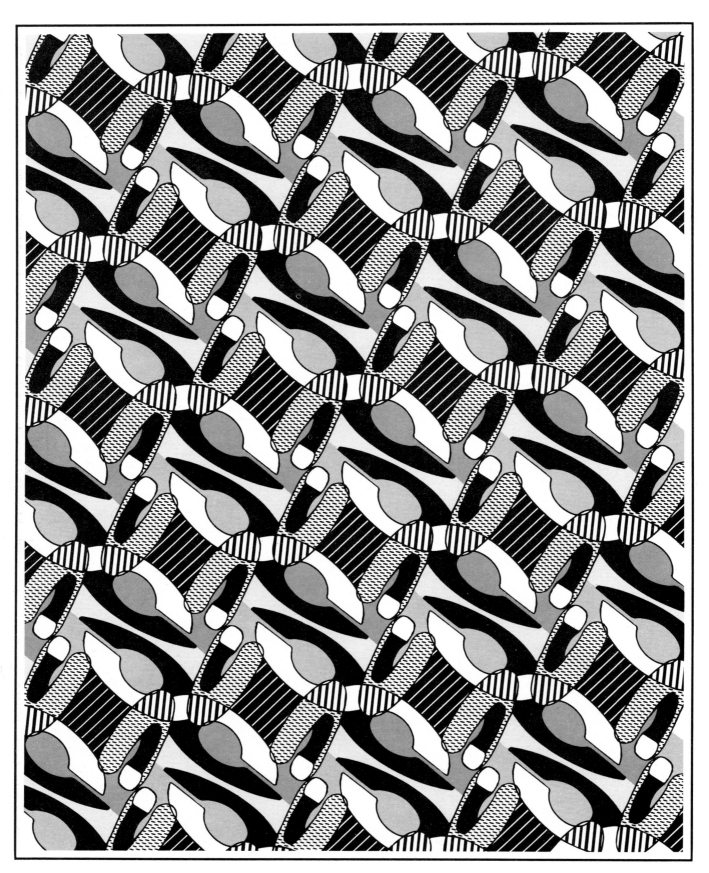

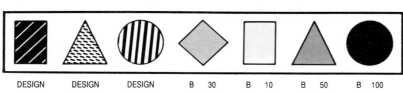

DESIGN   DESIGN   DESIGN   B 30   B 10   B 50   B 100

50

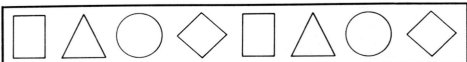

51

7

Any method of teaching must necessarily be mechanical to some degree as the results must be interpreted alike by all. "Design & Light" can be interpreted with definite accuracy by mechanical draftsmanship; yet these patterns should not be so perfect in balance or in symmetry that they become inert.

Anyone can create a simple pattern by outlining the silhouette forms of some object and its shadow. However, to create very interesting patterns, it is necessary to have some knowledge of drawing and a concept of form. Most of the patterns illustrated have their form or perspective and shade translated into color. Each main color plate is followed by a scale drawing and a photograph illustrating the method of creating that particular design, which is again interpreted in a variety of colored designs from the same scale drawing....

LockWasherDesign

A

B

C

D

E

F

PLATE 7-A. Lock Washer Design

G

53

54

Templet with Perspective

PLATE 7-B. Lock Washer Design, Photograph and Scale Drawing

8

Designs may be based either upon a horizontal or vertical line in which either the object or its shadow controls the pattern. Typical examples are Plates 11-A, B in which the vertical line of the object controls the pattern. If the shadows and objects are overlapped, the source loses its identity. An example of this case is Plate 15-A. This is illustrated by means of the scale drawing in Plate 15-B. It was done intentionally in order to present a combination of a rectangular object and a circular one. Then, too, there is no limit to the number of objects that may be used in creating a given pattern. If the design permits, either the object or the shadow may be eliminated when the other of the two is symmetric and permits its use, e.g. Plates 8-A, B. See also the illustration B on page 7. Here the lamp bulb has been used with the symmetrical part of the globe adjoining two stems of the lamp....

L a m p B u l b D e s i g n

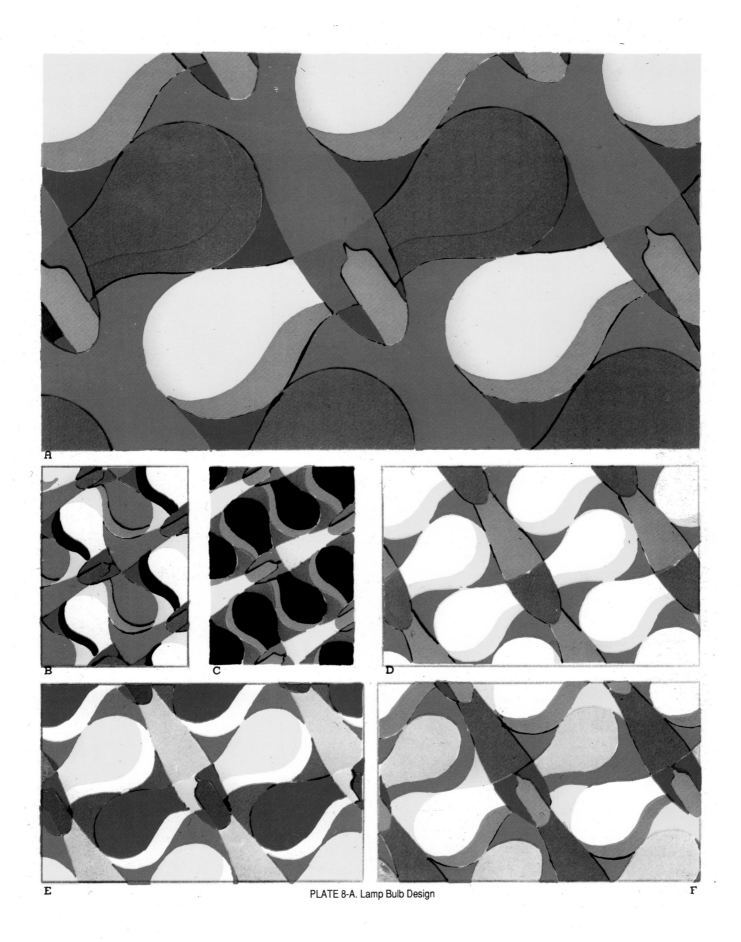

A

B   C   D

E   PLATE 8-A. Lamp Bulb Design   F

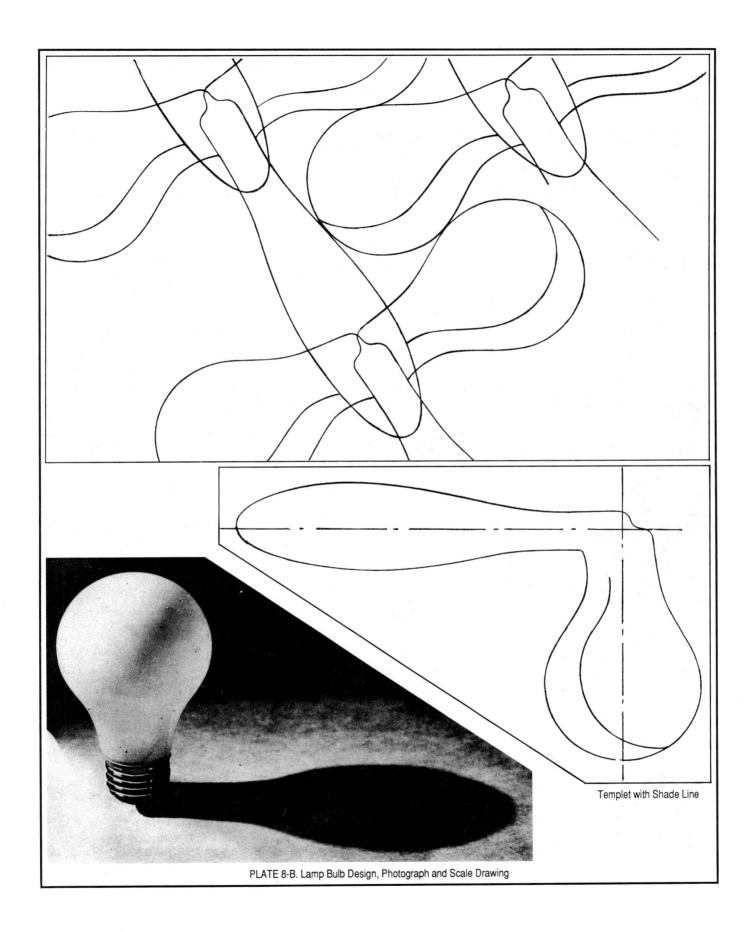

Templet with Shade Line

PLATE 8-B. Lamp Bulb Design, Photograph and Scale Drawing

9

To go to the opposite extreme, the object could have been eliminated entirely and the symmetric shadow colored.

A series of overlays could produce one object with two shadows or two objects with one shadow. For instance, the symmetry of the ping-pong ball in patterns on Plates 15-A, B could have become a basic line pattern with an overlay of the profile of the ping-pong ball, which would have shown one circular object with two rectangles. Examples of this are presented in the illustrations C, D, E, F, and G on page 7. For simple designs without perspective, a templet of the silhouette of the object and shadow may be used. The templet or silhouette may be made of paper, card board, or fiber board. It is also possible to simplify the perspective drawing by making a second templet of perspective lines, although it can readily be made free hand....

Lamp Bulb Design

A

B

C   D

E   F   PLATE 9-A. Lamp Bulb Design   G

61

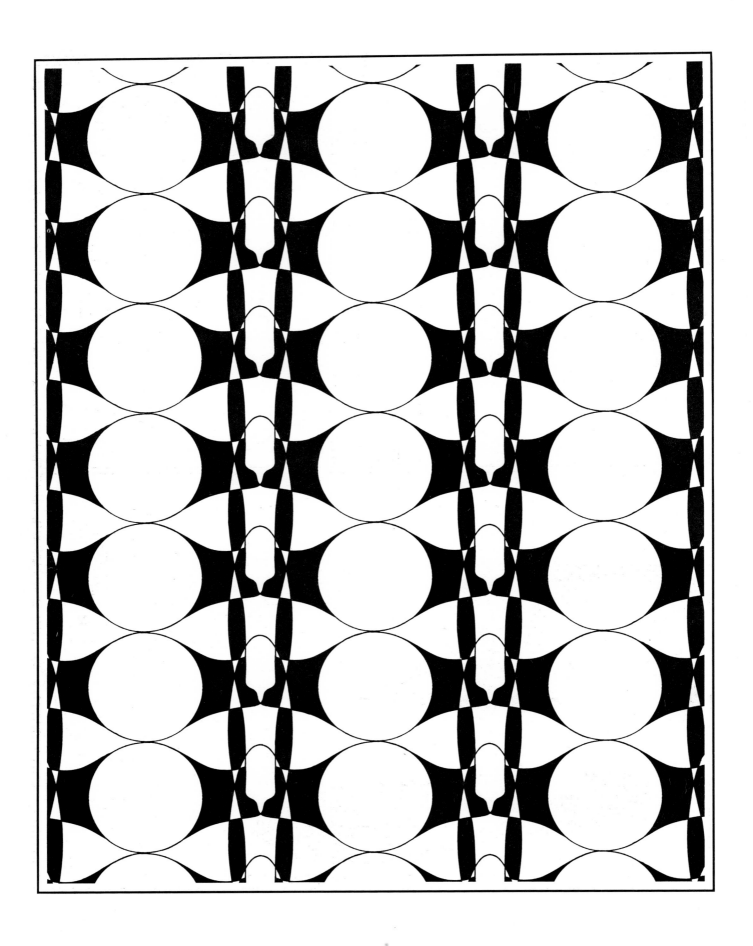

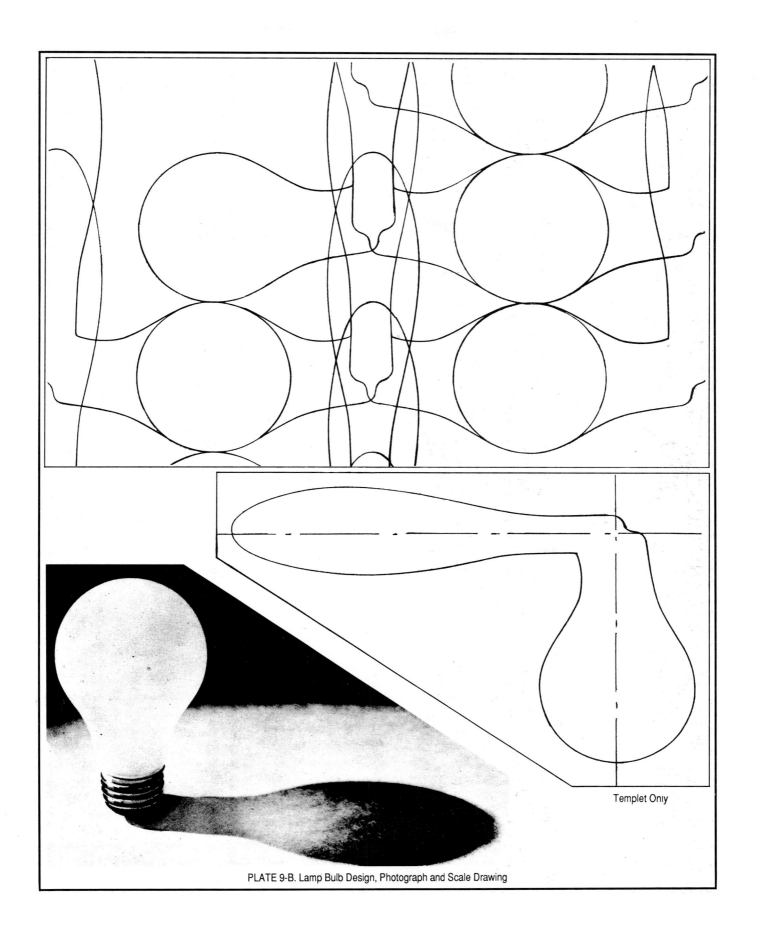

PLATE 9-B. Lamp Bulb Design, Photograph and Scale Drawing

Templet Only

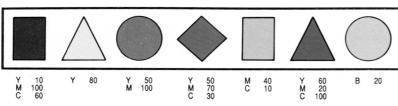

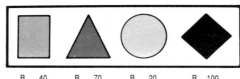

B   40   B   70   B   20   B   100

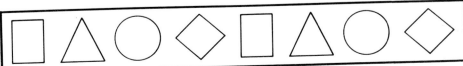

10

Solid objects will cast solid shadows. Objects with perforations will permit more liberal pattern and lend themselves more toward the abstract through the perforation of the shadows by light. An example of this is illustrated in the lock washer patterns on Plates 5-A, B and 6-A, B and 7-A, B.

Abstract patterns are created from segments of their sources. The slightest change in the position of the object or in the source of light will produce entirely different patterns. For instance, shadows cast on a plane at a diagonal to the horizon assume entirely different shapes from those cast on a plane perpendicular to the object.

The method, troughout the plates, has been presented in a simplified manner....

Lamp Bulb Design

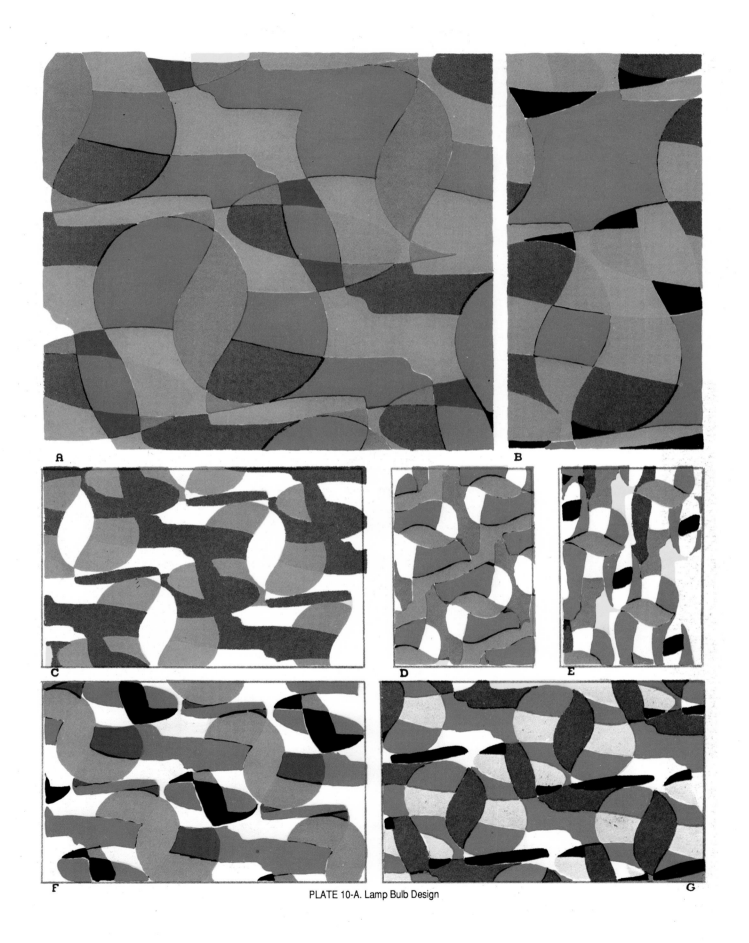

PLATE 10-A. Lamp Bulb Design

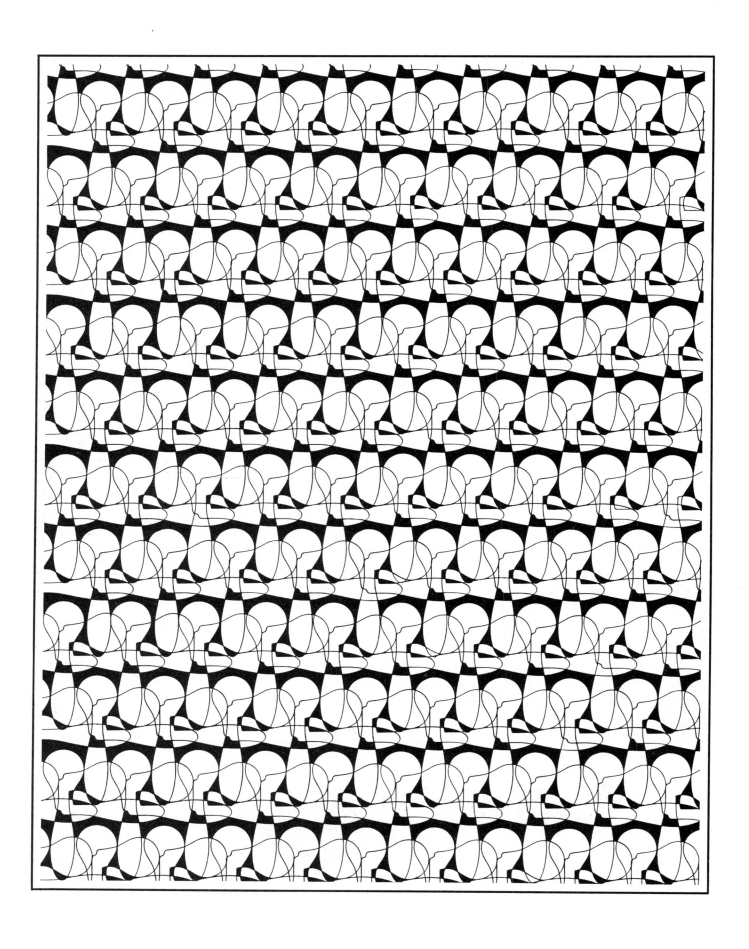

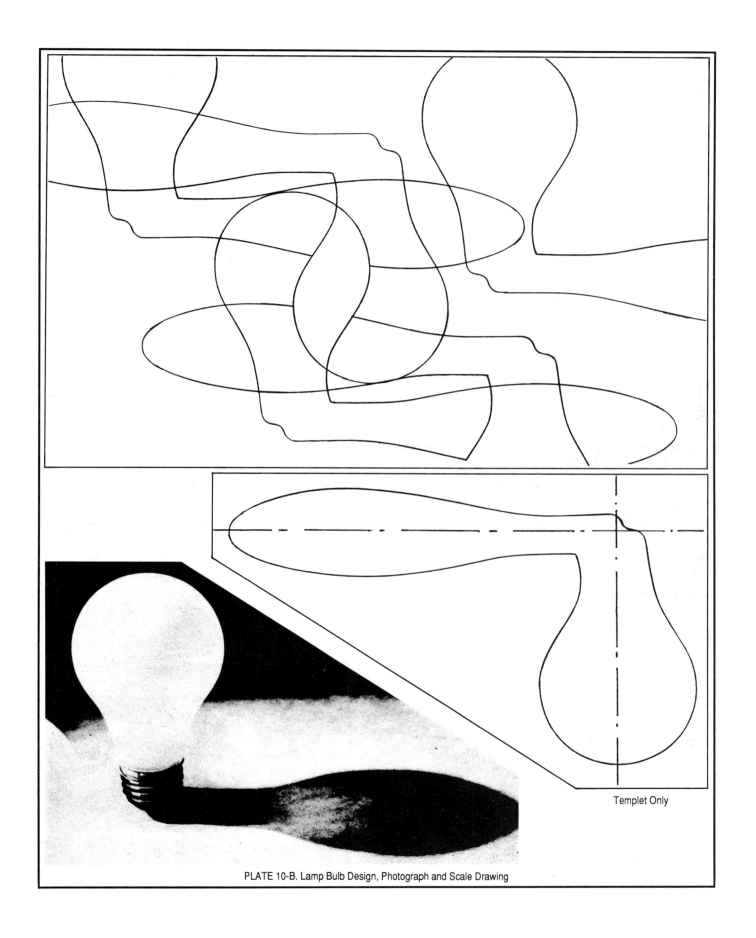

PLATE 10-B. Lamp Bulb Design, Photograph and Scale Drawing

Templet Only

11

The possibilities of creating more complex patterns by casting more than one shadow or by casting shadows on intersecting planes have not been attempted. The method will permit this complexity in line as well as in color. On the worksheet shown on page 6 there is a photograph suggesting further development along these lines in planes and reflections.

Another kind of elaboration is presented by the study of silhouettes or templets of plates without lines in perspective. Plates 10-A, B are simple patterns created entirely from the silhouette of the lamp bulb. There are no lines of perspective introduced. Notice the inversion of the templet, the staggered form, and the appropriate spacing in the overlays. Make a tracing of the templet and trace the developments of the form in the scale drawing....

InkWellDesign

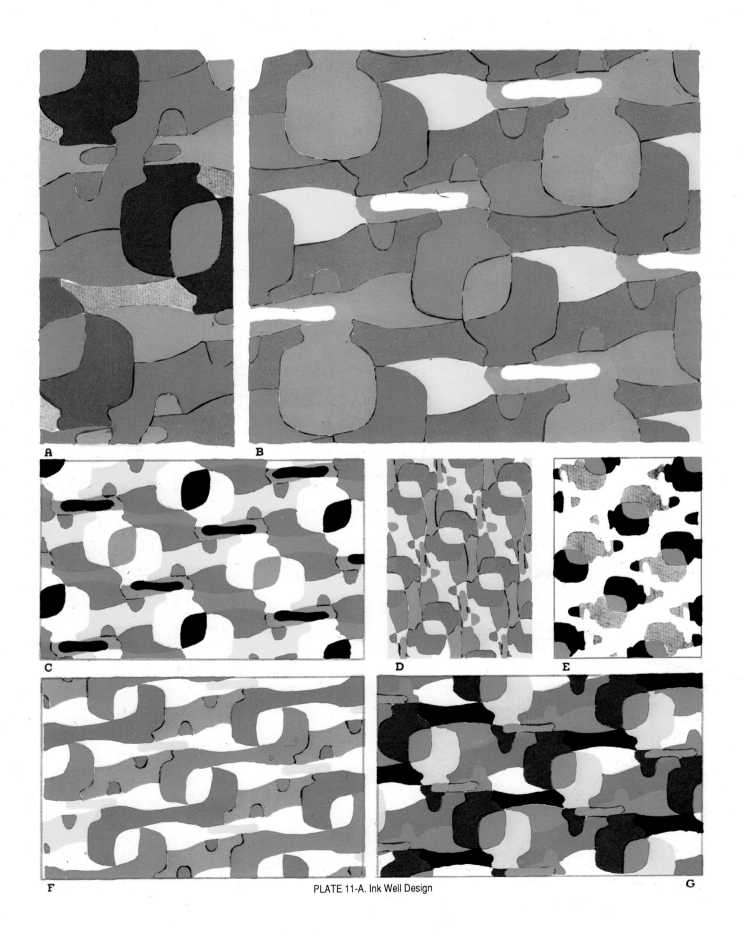

A   B   C   D   E   F

PLATE 11-A. Ink Well Design   G

73

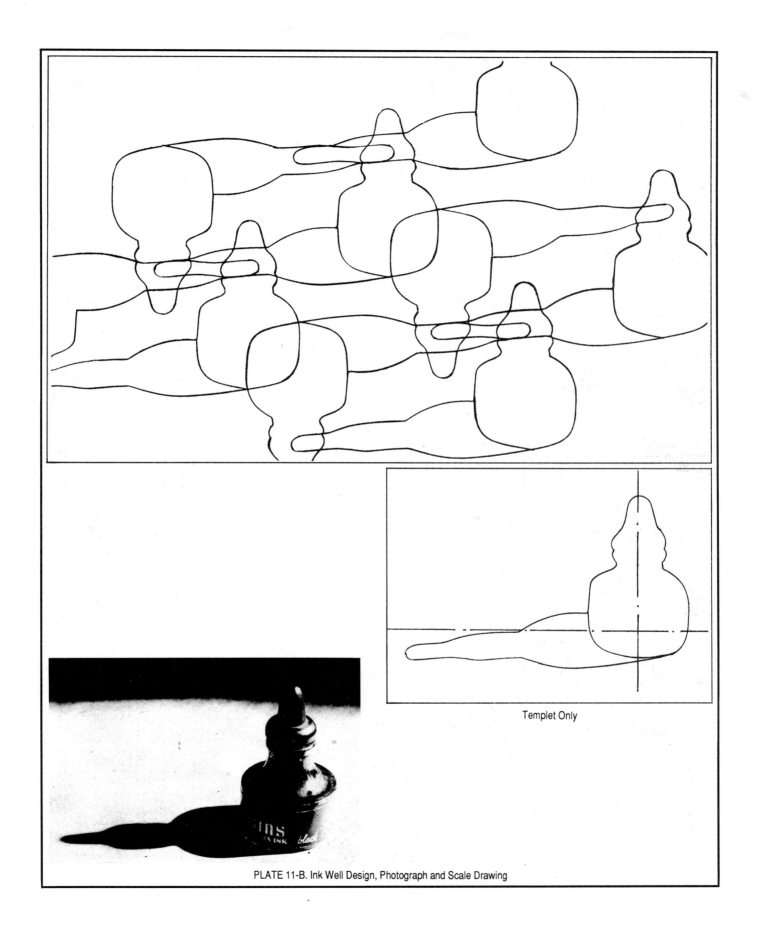

Templet Only

PLATE 11-B. Ink Well Design, Photograph and Scale Drawing

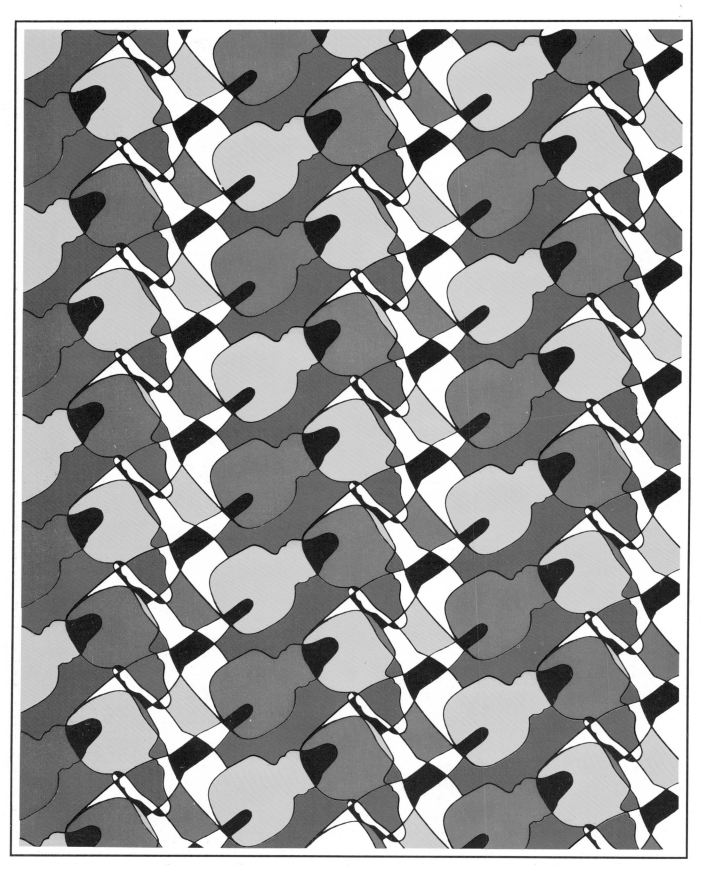

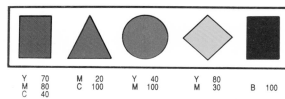

Y 70   M 20   Y 40   Y 80
M 80   C 100   M 100   M 30   B 100
C 40

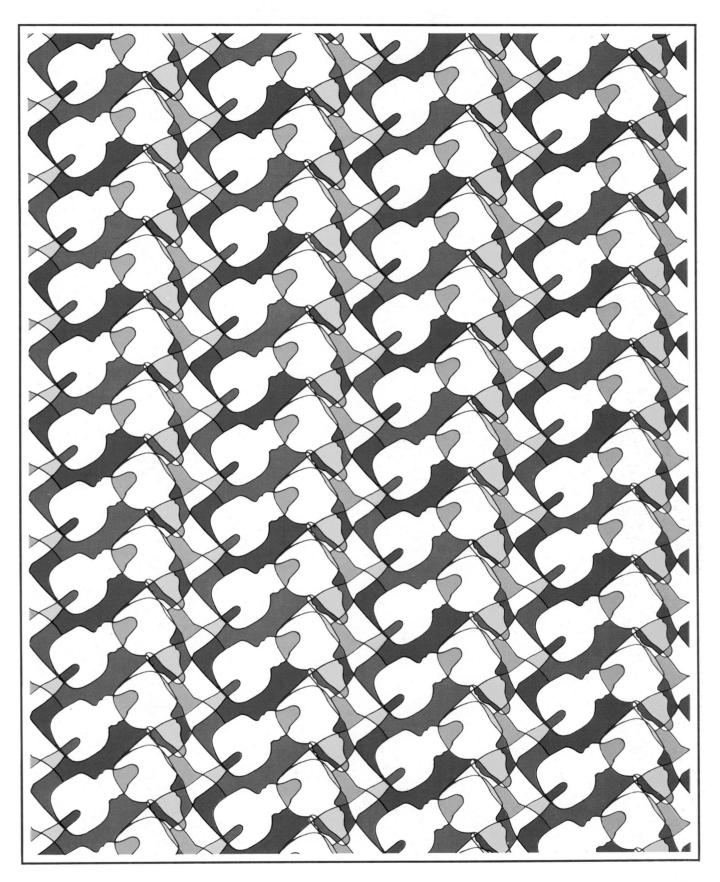

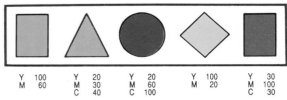

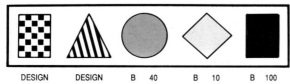

78

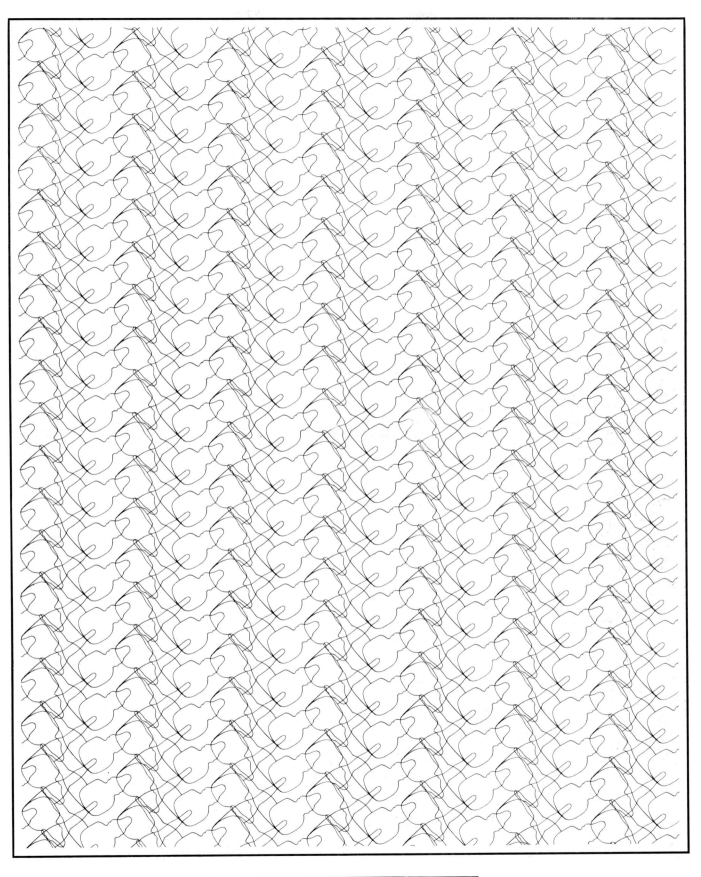

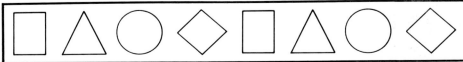

12

Patterns created on Plates 9-A, B represent the same templet as in Plates 10-A, B; it is made by the use of two shadows and one part of the bulb together with two stems of the lamp bulb. Turn now to the illustration B published on page 7 which is showing a thumb nail sketch explaining this part of the design.

Plates 8-A, B is another simple pattern created from the silhouette of the same lamp bulb. It has one shade line introduced. This shade line represents free-hand drawing in the pattern. So, in this instance, two lamp bulbs are used to create the pattern with the use of the shadow of only one lamp bulb. As used in the pattern, the silhouettes of the shadow mutually superimpose each other. See again the thumb nail sketch in Figure A on page 7....

TobaccoPipeDesign

PLATE 12-A. Tobacco Pipe Design

A

B   C

D   E

F   G

81

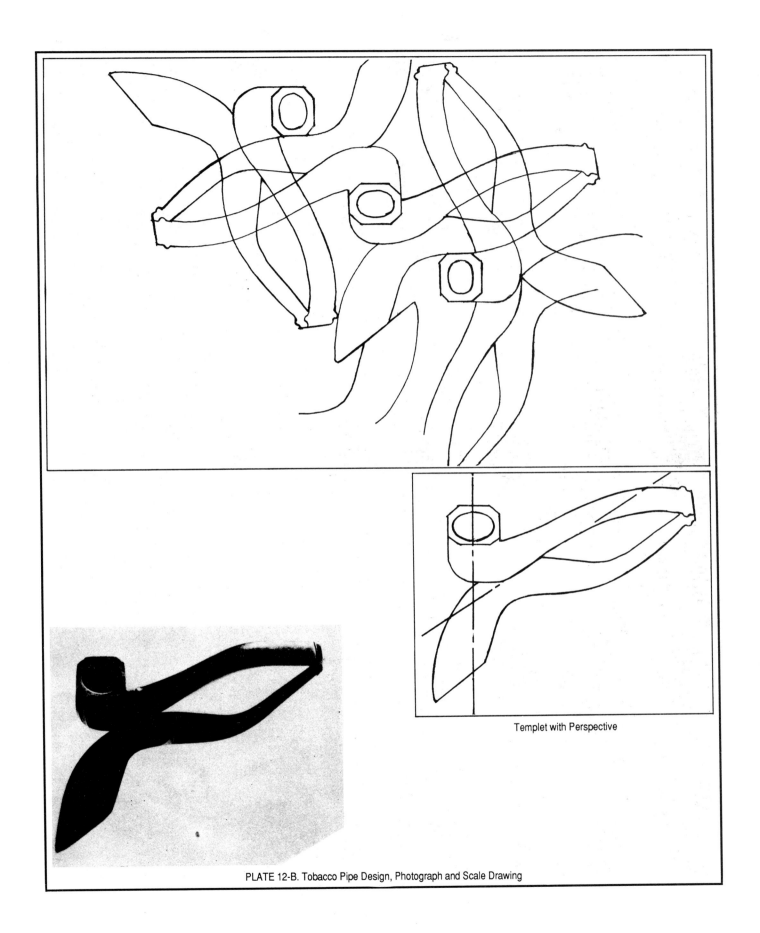

Templet with Perspective

PLATE 12-B. Tobacco Pipe Design, Photograph and Scale Drawing

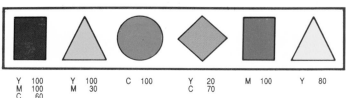

Y 100   Y 100   C 100   Y 20   M 100   Y 80
M 100   M 30   C 70
C 60

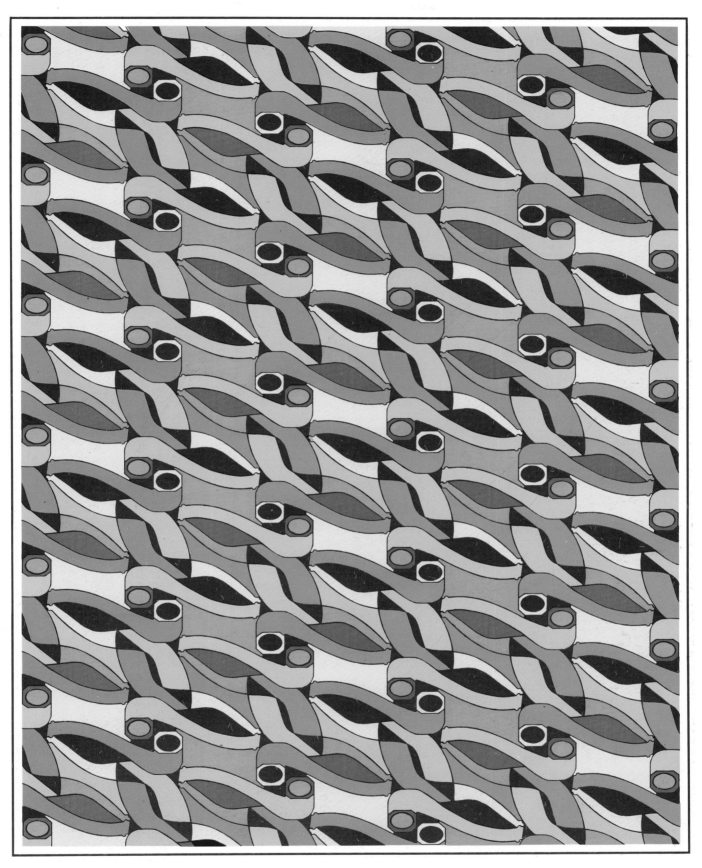

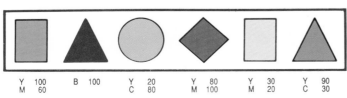

Y 100	B 100	Y 20	Y 80	Y 30	Y 90
M 60		C 80	M 100	M 20	C 30

DESIGN   DESIGN   DESIGN   DESIGN   DESIGN   B   30   B   100

86

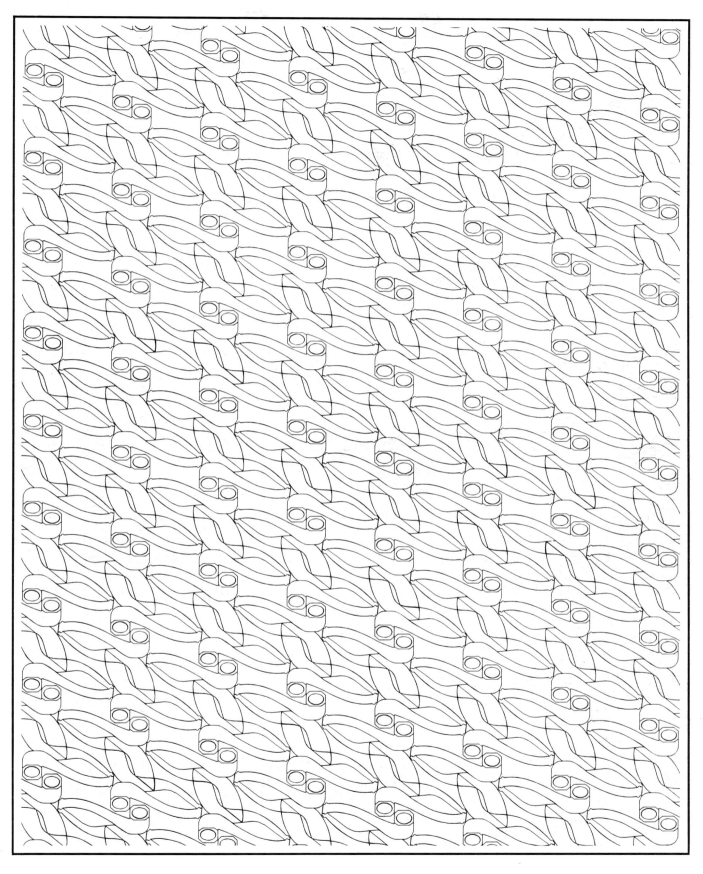

13

Plates 11-A, B are referred to as silhouettes or templets only; however, there is a shape line at the intersection of the shadow and the object. If this shape line were left out of the templet, it would make equally interesting patterns; but they would be entirely different form the present interpretation. This shape line must be drawn either free-hand, or a secondary templet may be made to serve the same purpose.

Plates 1-A, B represent a pattern created from a flat iron. The silhouette or templet has lines in perspective. A silhouette of the flat iron from the photograph will fit over the templet in the reversed outline. Patterns A, B, D, and E in color were created from the scale drawing on Plate 1-B. The templet in the design was used in inverted positions to make the pattern read in all directions....

M a t c h B o x D e s i g n

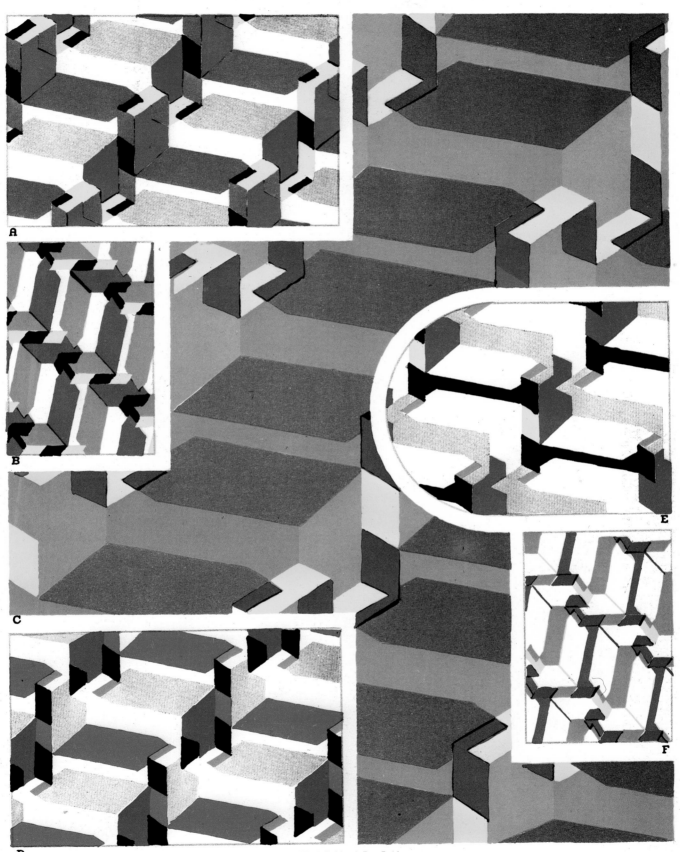

PLATE 13-A. Match Box Design

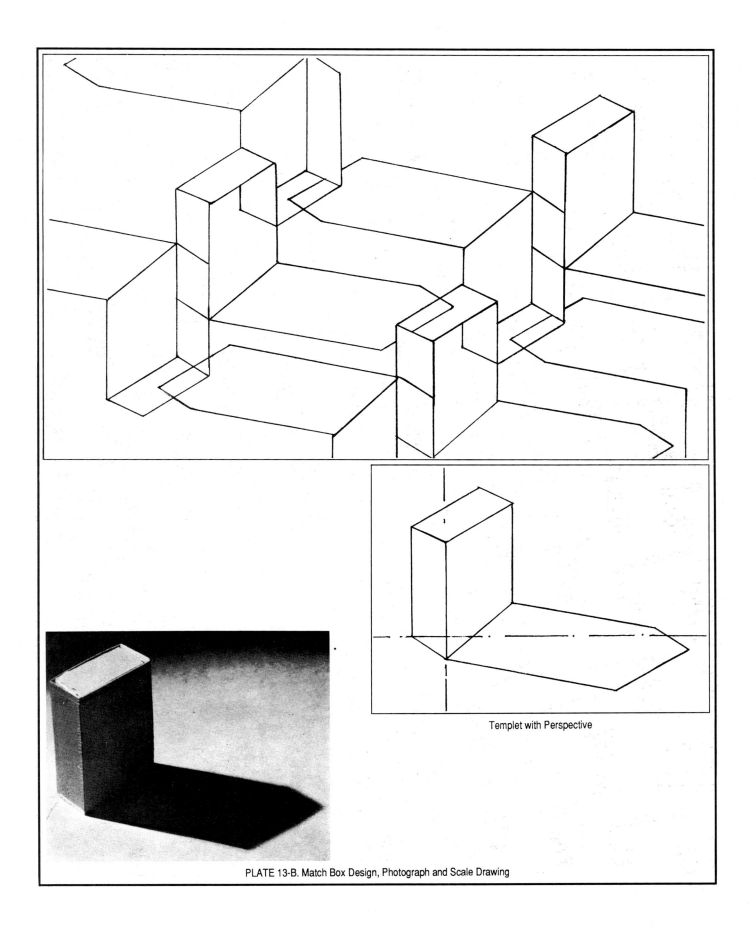

Templet with Perspective

PLATE 13-B. Match Box Design, Photograph and Scale Drawing

14

Figure C on color Plate 1-A represents a pattern created from the same templet as illustrated on Plate 1-B; however, this templet, while reversed in the pattern, was not inverted. This pattern reads only one way. There is no scale drawing of this particular pattern although it can readily be interpreted from the templet. Most patterns in the present book read in all directions. An outstanding example of a pattern created one way is that of the illustration of the hats; see Plates 4-A, B. The hat in the scale drawing and in the color plate was at no time inverted. In the abstract patterns of Plate 4-A, Figures B and F, the hats virtually disappear; and the pattern reads in all directions. Most of the other patterns on the various plates are read in all directions through the inversion of the templet. When the templet is inverted, the object and the shadow are automatically inverted with it....

M a t c h B o x D e s i g n

PLATE 14-A. Match Box Design

93

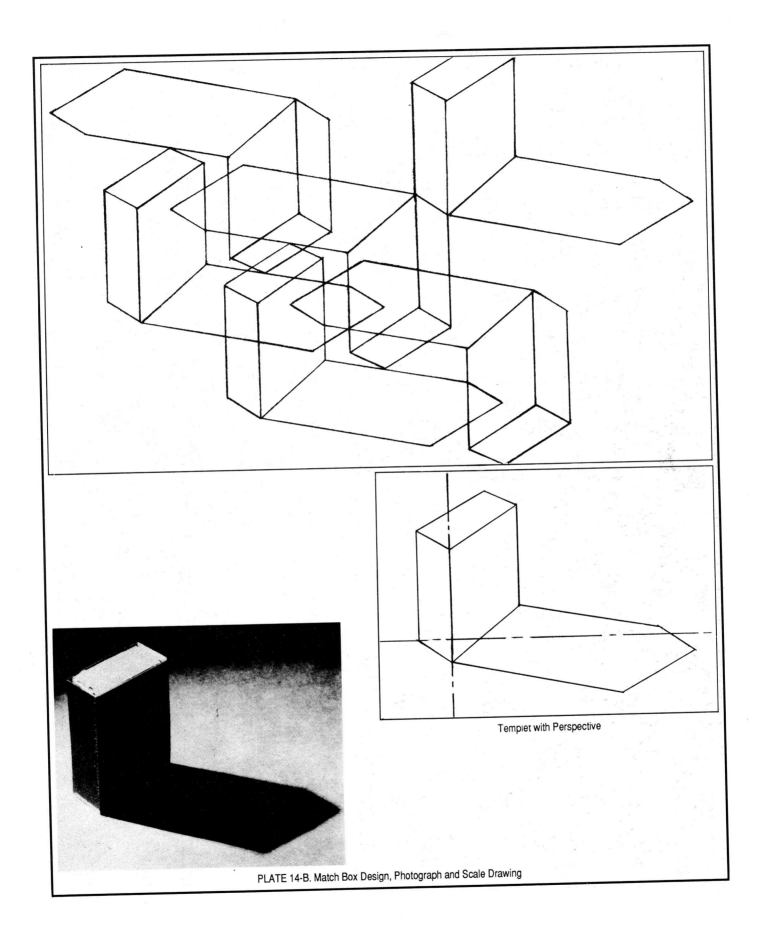

Templet with Perspective

PLATE 14-B. Match Box Design, Photograph and Scale Drawing

95

15

For study in color, place transparent paper over any of the scale drawings and apply color from crayons, water color or oil. In this manner the scale drawings may be interpreted in forms of color pattern other than those published. The same method should apply to any original pattern created. It allows for innumerable color studies before applying color definitely to the original drawing. Another way would be to photostat the original drawing and make color studies on the photostats. Photostats were used in producing the plates for the publication. Incidentally, it allowed for the many reductions of the same pattern, which again were translated into a variety of color patterns.

Each plate represents patterns created from one scale drawing. There is a full size colored pattern supplemented with numerous studies in color and in black and white.

M a t c h B o x B a l l D e s i g n

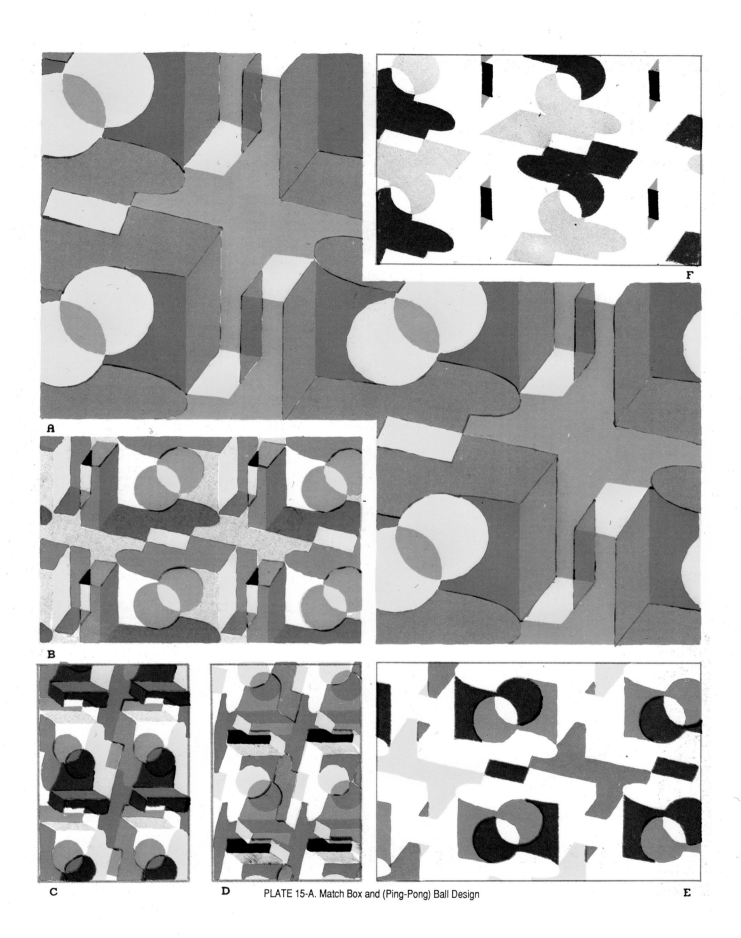

PLATE 15-A. Match Box and (Ping-Pong) Ball Design

A

B

C

D

E

F

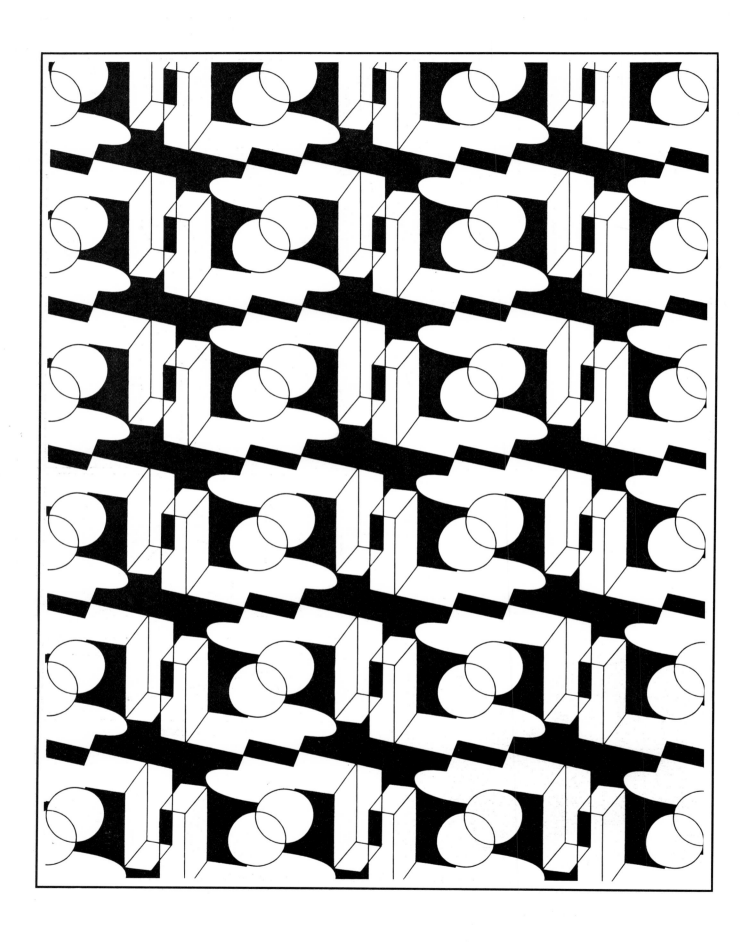

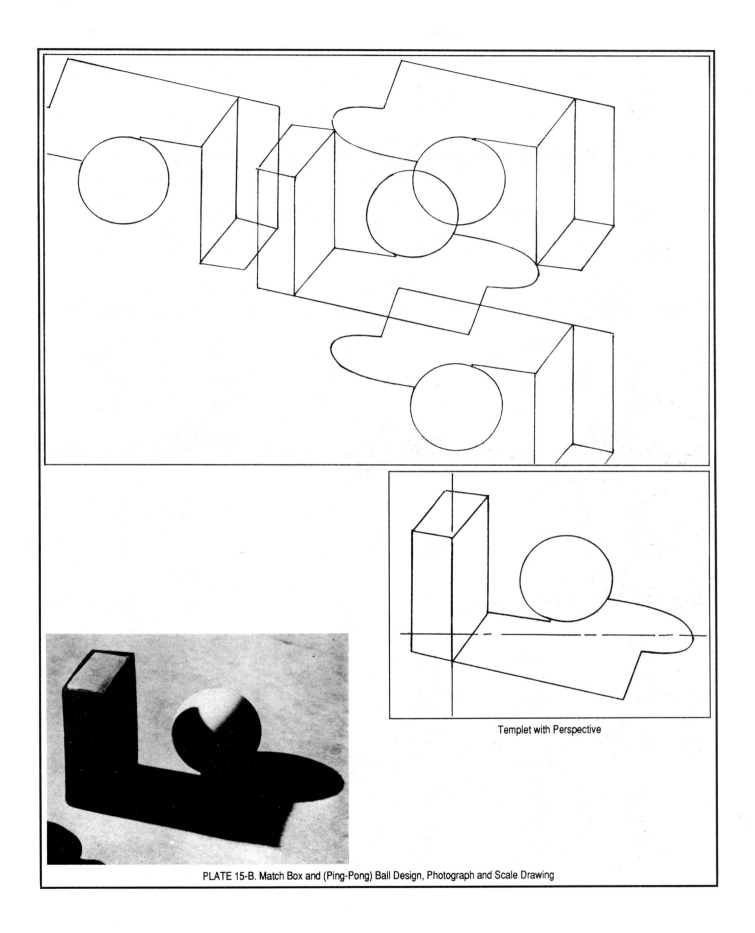

Templet with Perspective

PLATE 15-B. Match Box and (Ping-Pong) Ball Design, Photograph and Scale Drawing

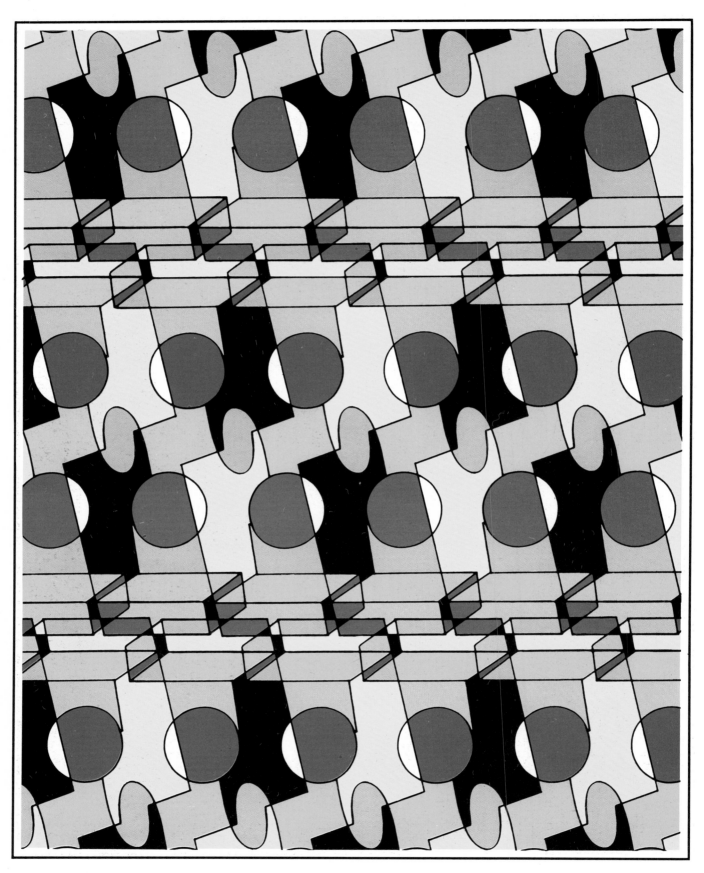

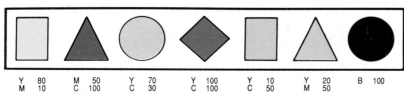

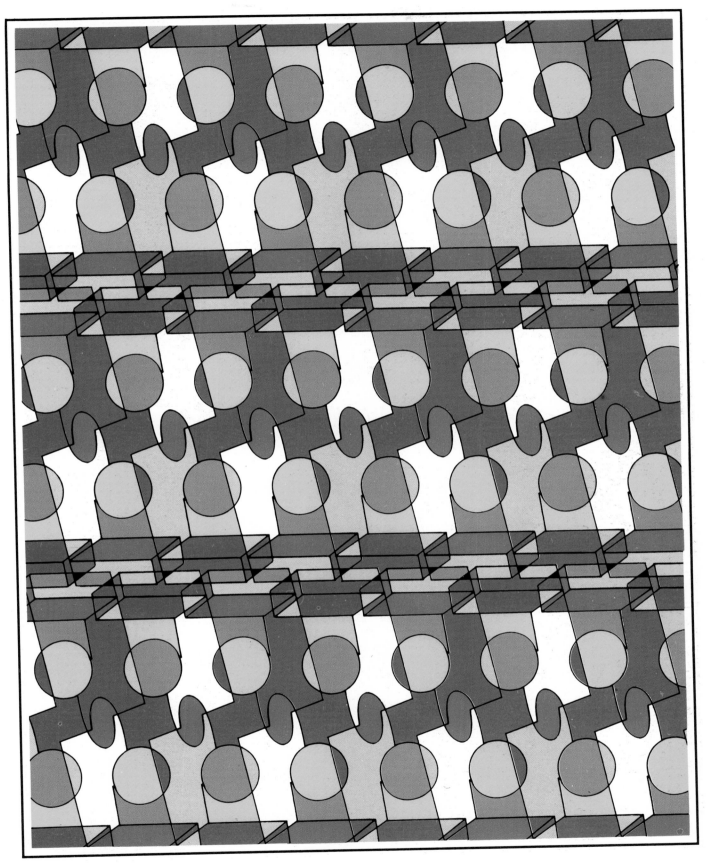

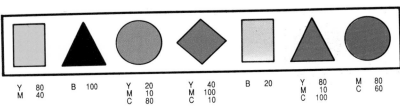

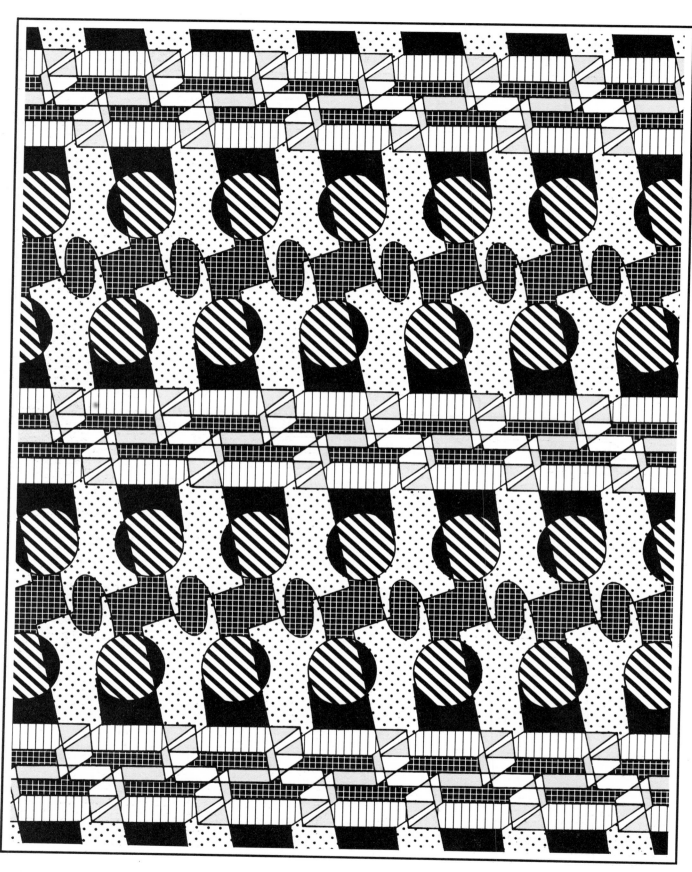

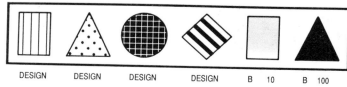

DESIGN   DESIGN   DESIGN   DESIGN   B   10   B   100

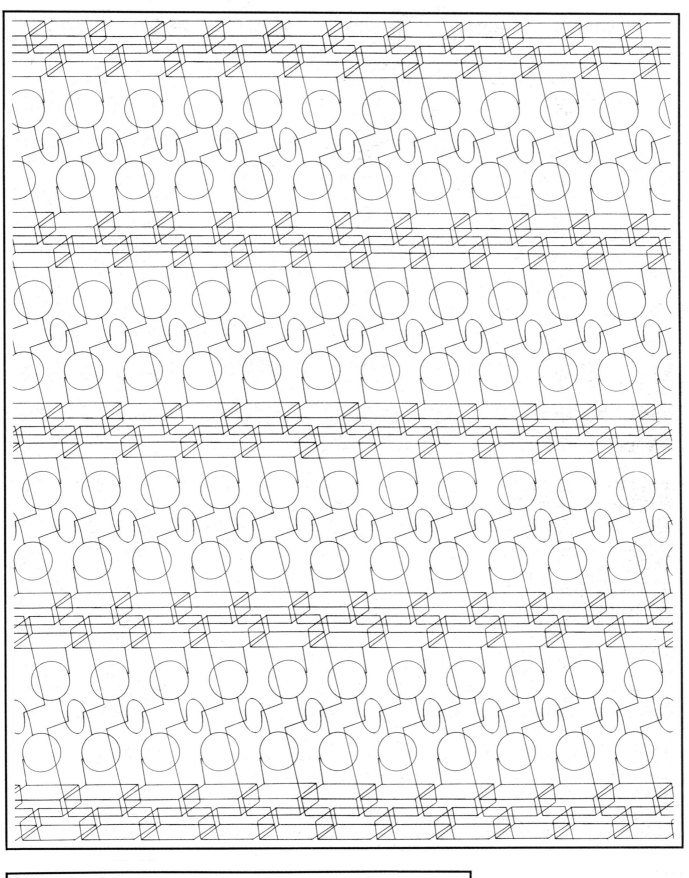

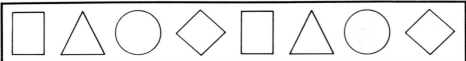

BEL
VEDERE

SIMPLY THE BEST

EDITION
BELVEDERE

DESIGN
BOOKS

MADE
IN
ITALY

Design Club

FASHION TEXTILES GRAPHIC DESIGN
PHOTOGRAPHY LAYOUT DECORATION
ADVERTISING STYLING ILLUSTRATION
ORNAMENTS INTERIOR ARCHITECTURE

Good Design Books are hard to find. It takes you time and money to get the right images & references you need for your work. But now you can have it all more easily. Choose simply the best in its field: Belvedere-Design-Books, "made in Italy". Go, and ask for the DESIGN CLUB, and you will get a special offer (free of charge) immediately. It will surprise you.

E' difficile trovare buoni design books. Ci vuole tempo e denaro per avere le immagini e le idee giuste. Ma adesso è tutto più facile. Scegliete solamente il meglio: i Belvedere-Design-Books, "made in Italy". Chiedete del DESIGN-CLUB e avrete subito & gratis delle offerte eccezionali che vi sorprenderanno.

Gute Designbücher sind schwierig zu finden. Es erfordert oft viel Zeit und Geld, um an die richtigen Ideen & Vorlagen zu gelangen. Doch jetzt ist alles viel leichter. Wählen Sie einfach das Beste: Belvedere-Design-Books, "made in Italy". Erkundigen Sie sich nach dem DESIGN-CLUB und Sie werden unverzüglich & kostenlos ein Spezial-Angebot erhalten, das Sie überraschen wird.

BELVEDERE

DESIGNER'S NOTEBOOK

28

COLLEGE LIBRARY

SOMERSET COLLEGE OF ARTS AND TECHNOLOGY
Wellington Road, Taunton, Somerset TA1 5AX
(283403 ext 236)

This book is due for return on or before the last date shown below.

BELVEDERE